For my grandmother, Sophia Morton – F.H.

LADYBIRD BOOKS, INC.
Auburn, Maine 04210 U.S.A.
© LADYBIRD BOOKS LTD 1990
Loughborough, Leicestershire, England

Printed in England

Wise King Solomon

Retold by Fern Howard
Illustrated by Lydia Halverson

Ladybird Books

David, the king of Israel, was growing old. He called
his son Solomon to his side. "When I die, you will be
king," David said. "Rule well, and keep God's
commandments. You will prosper, and our
descendants will rule Israel forever."

Soon David died, and Solomon became king. Solomon loved the Lord and did as David had told him, and his kingdom prospered.

Solomon often sacrificed animals and burned incense as offerings to the Lord.

One time he went to the great altar at Gibeon and made a thousand burnt offerings to the Lord. That night, he had a dream. In his dream, the Lord appeared and told Solomon to ask for anything he wanted, and he would have it.

Solomon replied, "Even though I am now king, I am not always sure what to do. Please give me wisdom, so that I will know right from wrong and always be a good king."

The Lord was pleased that Solomon had asked for wisdom instead of riches or long life. He told Solomon, "Yes, you will be the wisest man who ever lived and have wealth and honor, too! And if you follow me, as your father did, you will have a long life."

Soon afterward, two women came to King Solomon and asked him to settle an argument. The two women had a baby with them, and each woman claimed the child was hers.

"We both live in the same house," the first woman explained, "and we both gave birth to sons. One night, this woman's baby died. She came to where my baby and I were sleeping, and she stole my son and put her baby in his place.

"In the morning," the woman said, "I thought my son had died. But when I walked into the daylight, I understood right away what had happened."

"That's not true!" the other woman interrupted.
"The dead child is hers, and the living child is mine!"
So they argued in front of the king.

King Solomon said, "Both of you say the child who
lives is her own, and the dead child belongs to the
other. All right. I have an answer. Bring me a
sword."

When the sword was brought, King Solomon said, "The answer is simple. Divide the child in two, and give half to each mother."

"This solution is fair," said the second woman to the king. "The child will not be hers or mine. Cut him in two!"

"No, no!" said the first woman. "Give her the child if you must. But please do not kill him!"

They waited for the king to give the order. But King Solomon said, "Give the baby to the woman who wants him to live, for she is his true mother!"